Lao-Tzu, or The Way of the Dragon

Lao-Tzu,
or The Way of the Dragon

Narrated by
Miriam Henke

Illustrated by
Jérôme Meyer-Bisch

Translated by
Jordan Lee Schnee

Plato & Co.
diaphanes

One warm, cloudless night during the Zhou dynasty, a comet departed from a far-off planet and streaked past Earth, leaving a trail of stars in its wake. A young Chinese woman was sitting outside her hut watching the sky.

Awed by the heavens, she swallowed the pit of the plum she was eating. From life comes life; this is what change is. In the next year she gave birth to a baby. He looked like an old man and because of his long ears he was named Li-Tan.

As he grew up, Li-Tan proved to be a very smart boy.
He did not let himself get bested by indecision, and would
not get sucked in by impatience. When he was praised for
his peaceful and modest ways, he would answer:

"The path we see is not the Way."

"No doubt about it," the villagers said, "this child is
a dragon's son."

Li-Tan smiled when he heard the villagers:

"In your eyes I am the son of that majestic creature whose dark form unfurls to ride the clouds? People like you always exaggerate. The humility of the earth provides more stability than the ambition of heaven."

I don't know which family the dragon belongs to. In our *Celestial Treasure Encyclopedia of Beneficent Teachings*, I found the following classification of animals:

> Animals that belong to the Emperor
> Animals kept in jars
> Tame animals
> Suckling pigs
> Mermaids
> Imaginary animals
> Stray dogs
> Crazy animals
> Uncountable creatures
> Animals drawn with very thin paint brushes
> Animals who broke the water jar
> Ones that, from far away, look like flies

Not only are there no dragons in this list, but what vanity to want to impose order upon everything! Later on people will think of this classification as severely lacking, even though it seems so apt to us today."

And so Li-Tan's name was changed to Lao-Tzu, which means "Old Sage."

Lao-Tzu loved deciphering the endless book of the world. Walking along the rice fields, in the shadow of boulders surrounded by gingko and white mulberry trees, across the brilliant green terraces and steep embankments, he sometimes ranged as far as the northern heights. The snowy peaks showed him his own insignificance among the 10,000 other creatures that populate the universe.

The simple facts of life never ceased to amaze Lao-Tzu.
He daydreamed while watching the farmers:

"Thirty slats come out of a plow, but it's thanks to the spaces
between them that the plow works. And drinking glasses—it's
the empty space inside that counts. And how could you put
doors and windows on a house without it being hollow?
So the existence of a thing comes from a fullness, but its
use comes from its emptiness."

Lao-Tzu's schoolmates liked his ruminations. Many did
not exactly understand them, but took them up because
they jostled the Ancients' doctrines. The young fools were
exuberant, bubbling—like spurting mountain springs.

Lao-Tzu became an archivist and astrologer in the imperial court of Luoyang, in Henan province. Along with a few disciples, he was put in charge of the newly established imperial library. Emperor Pingwang had taken it upon himself to modernize the empire, moving the capital to Luoyang and increasing the number of institutions and functionaries.

In reality the kingdom had found itself cut up into seven provinces. Emperor Pingwang had placed an allied prince at the head of each. When one of the princes died, his province was split between his sons, then between their sons. Eventually the empire consisted of many little coexisting kingdoms. The emperor ruled by maintaining their rivalries, as if lying in bed, his feet gnawed by small insects.

Lao-Tzu observed the intrigues of the doomed court from his library window. Sometimes he saw an old man with a deeply lined face walking in the imperial gardens among the chrysanthemums and butterflies.

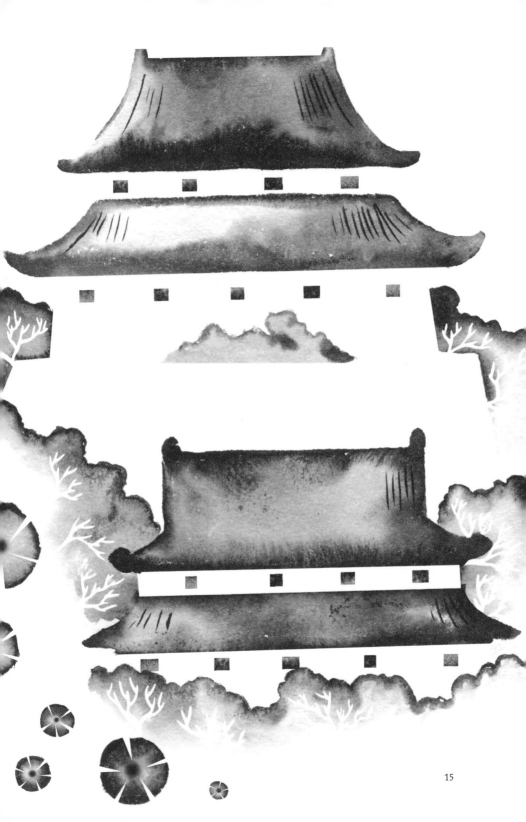

15

The venerable Confucius was an advisor to the emperor, and Lao-Tzu could deduce the source of his sadness. He understood that Pingwang was a powerful man but weak in spirit. He ruled others, but did not know how to rule himself. He always fell victim to his own impatience, and this led him to make foolish and sometimes dangerous decisions.

"A man who is truly strong can face the rhinoceros and the tiger," thought Lao-Tzu, "because he has abandoned his desires, and therefore does not fear death. But a man governed by perpetual anxiety is weak."

Tea leaves slowly unfold in seething water. Emperor Pingwang was the opposite. His impatience would eventually be his downfall. Tea leaves can infuse water only when the time is right, after having dried in the sun. This is the way of all things—you have to wait for the right moment. A prince needs to recognize when to influence his subjects by plying them with gifts. This is not what was happening in China. Pingwang was a bustling yet ineffective person, and his empire was like a ripe fruit left uneaten.

One day ancient Confucius went to the Imperial Library, where he was received by Lao-Tzu, who courteously fetched Confucius the works he wished to consult. Confucius then began to interpret *The Annals of Spring and Autumn* with unparalleled grace and intelligence. He spoke of the wisdom of past emperors, the necessity of moral education for the people, and confided the hope he placed in the generosity and justice of human nature to Lao-Tzu.

Lao-Tzu bowed slightly:

"Benevolence and lordly piety are not natural states. They were created by people," he replied.

Confucius bowed in turn:

"Who could live among the birds and wild animals without rules and laws? Who wouldn't want to make perfect order reign by the harmony of the middle ground?"

"The order of things," replied Lao-Tzu, "comes before this harmony. Someone with a bowl of water is worth less than someone who can go without one. A sharpened sword can't keep its edge forever. A room full of gold and jade can't be kept for eternity."

Confucius lit up with a smile. No one had ever spoken like that before:

"If all human actions lead to disharmony, then should we resort to absolute inaction?" he asked.

"The Way of heaven," replied Lao-Tzu, "is not mere inaction, but active inaction: to act according to the natural order of things. Water is the weakest of the elements, yet it manages to clear a path, and once its work is done it pulls back. The Way is like water."

"So where is the path to this Way?" inquired Confucius.

Lao-Tzu then repeated, as if saying it to himself:

"The path we see is not the Way. I can't show you the Way, and you can't follow it."

These words shook ancient Confucius. For a whole month he did not speak a word. Even music, which he had so appreciated, was not able to distract him. Was it possible, as Lao-Tzu had implied, that human justice did not exist? That brotherly love, respect for one's elders, and honesty would not be able to reestablish order?

Meanwhile the empire descended further into corruption. Lao-Tzu, for his part, decided to go off in search of the Way, far from the haphazard names which people had used to encase the manifestations of things.

Emperor Pingwang was surprised when Lao-Tzu gave up
his high position for a life of poverty and wandering:

"Oh my faithful servant, but how I have spoiled you!
What more could you want?"

Lao-Tzu paid his respects to the emperor, saying:

"We attach too much importance to ourselves, and we grow complacent with the admiration of others. Why seek fame, fortune, or power? Tigers and leopards are hunted for their beauty, monkeys are captured for their dexterity, and dogs are raised to guard yaks. Those who amasses wealth make their peers uncomfortable and feed anxiety in their own hearts. Those who aspire to fame can be disgraced. Titles and riches trap people in themselves. The sage, however, breaks free from the limits of the self to follow the Way of the universe, and find themselves in infinity."

Returning to the library, Lao-Tzu announced his plan to leave to his followers. He did not tell them where he wanted to go, just saying he would head west. His disciples felt abandoned:

"Master," they said, "for years you have taught us to follow the eternal Way. Isn't it the same in the west as in the emperor's court? Why do you want to leave us if we love you?"

Lao-Tzu answered them:

"Respecting your parents is easier than loving them, which is easier than forgetting them, which is easier than being forgotten yourself. Your attempts to be virtuous and loyal to your master compromise your natural virtues. Those who possess supreme honor are above all the honors in the kingdom; those who possess supreme wealth are above all material riches; those who possess supreme aspiration are above reputation and praise. This is why the Way is unalterable."

There were many who wanted to follow the great sage, but like a fox crossing a river without getting its tail wet, Lao-Tzu pulled off a great trick. Perched on the back of a water buffalo, he disappeared step after step into the forest. Alone on the road, he found himself on the verge of a new beginning.

Next morning, a milky dawn began to float up through the blackness of the still-dark sky. The world's shapes had yet to decide what they wanted to be. Soon the silver edges of the clouds began to glitter in the day's first rays, then melted in the sun. The sounds of the night dissipated. Relieved of the burdens of the court, Lao-Tzu was aware of his limbs shaking off their torpor. Nature was immutable, destiny irrevocable, like the seasons' turning.

"Let's go!" he said to the water buffalo. "Forward march! Let nothing fall across the Way! The Way makes everything possible. Without the Way, nothing is possible!"

As the seasons passed, Lao-Tzu crossed the changing landscapes of the vast empire. It seemed to him that he was taking in the world for the first time. The utter beauty of cows and horses crossing his path was a manifestation of a marvelous intelligence. Their four legs and shining coats had come from the heavens, but the horse's bridle and the ring in the cow's nose had been put there by people. Doing so was despicable because it troubled the natural order of things.

Many years passed. Many swallows, many orioles followed Lao-Tzu on his path between heaven and earth.

One hot afternoon, after leaving a scorching valley, Lao-Tzu and his buffalo climbed a rocky trail, looking for shade. As they went higher, a noise came to them. It could barely be heard but was all the more threatening for it.
Lao-Tzu recognized the neighing, the shouted orders followed by the cold clanking of swords. The arrows' whistling paralleled the sound of the spirits crying.

Lao-Tzu's water buffalo flattened his ears, and seemed to look at him with his big black eyes before risking a step forward along the ledge. On the other side of the mountain, Lao-Tzu saw two armies confronting each other. The horses' hooves had whipped the dust into a cyclone, wrapping the warriors in an impenetrable veil. The battle's contours were blurred by the distance, but the metallic smell of blood made it very real. The two kings' attempt to change destiny through armed force caused an immense sadness within Lao-Tzu. Before night fell, many men would die for a cause that was not of the smallest importance in the serene to-and-fro of the universe.

"Weapons are the tools of sadness, despicable to those who respect life. Whoever's spirit is inhabited by murder has already given up life," thought Lao-Tzu.

In the late afternoon the sky grew dark with clouds in
menacing shapes, and soon the first booms of the storm rang
out. The squall did not last long. It reminded Lao-Tzu of the
discourses of the high functionaries at the Imperial Court.
Squalls and showers are violent but short-lived, while the sky
and the earth are eternal.

The point was to not loose yourself in words looking for the
Way, but to surrender yourself to it. The branches above him
dripped steadily, and the water buffalo went along lightly,
a witness to the good omen.

As evening fell, Lao-Tzu stopped in a clearing surrounded by bamboo. He leisurely inhaled the aroma of fresh soil that came with the night. He lay against his buffalo's velvety flank, his eyes turned towards the sky. Like the dragon rising in the springtime after hibernating in the abysses, sleep brought Lao-Tzu towards unexplored expanses.

The milky moon lit up the hills. As he floated between emptiness and being, Lao-Tzu flew over their flowery ridges. In the heavens he thought he could make out the Way and began walking on powdery clouds, where only the birds come and go.

Little by little, the clouds solidified under Lao-Tzu's feet into a strangely soft substance. He reached the western gate. There the colors seemed lighter.

A road flanked by pines wound into the hills, ten thousand leagues away from the armies of ancient emperors. As he padded through the pine needles that danced around his feet, Lao-Tzu moved into the rocky shadows. Beneath a white willow, an old woman was sitting upon a tuft of grass. She was holding a pitcher. Lao-Tzu addressed her politely, inquiring where the path led. The old woman stared at him with her huge eyes and answered in a screeching voice that sounded like dry, windblown leaves:

"I am the spirit of the river, and this path doesn't go anywhere."

"What river?" Lao-Tzu asked.

"I keep the river locked in my pitcher, but I can release it any moment. The river is the Way. In following the Way, you will reach utmost virtue, which is like a tonic for all beings and cuts through all, yet causes no pain."

Lao-Tzu followed the path across ridges that were buffeted by spring and autumn winds. Finally, he reached the entrance to a cave that was guarded by a golden monkey.

Oh Lao-Tzu, I've been waiting for you
for nearly a half a century. Imagine
how bored I must be, all alone
in front of this cave!
You don't run into anyone here. My last
conversation was some twenty years ago.
With a porcupine.

Then the monkey bounded into the darkness, only to reappear a moment later beside the sage, apparently beckoning to be followed.

As they descended into the cave, the monkey, overjoyed at having a friend, did pirouettes and told fables:

Have you ever heard of the frog at the bottom
of the well? She said to the sea turtle:
"I love it here. I get out, jump up onto the edge, go back down
to the bottom, take a rest in a hole. When I dive down, the water supports me,
and my legs plunge into the mud. All the way up
to my ankles! The larvae, mosquitos, and crabs
that live around me can't compare. If you have the waters of a well,
it's all there. It can't be beat!"
Then the sea turtle described the ocean to the frog:
"A thousand leagues can't measure its distance; a thousand fathoms can't
comprise its depths. The great joy of the sea is that it's unchanging, no matter
how much water pours in, or evaporates off. Waves of love and hate
come and go, but the calm of the sea never runs out."
Imagine the frog's reaction! Human knowledge is limited. Like the frog's
satisfaction, your theories, your subtle notions, your wisdom
will only last for a while.

At the end of a vast labyrinth of tunnels, Lao-Tzu and the golden monkey reached an underground lake. Bounding ahead, the monkey motioned for to Lao-Tzu to look. In the middle of the lake, heralded by ripples, a huge lotus bud was emerging from the black water. It opened its silky petals one by one. The iridescent colors reflected on the cave walls. Lao-Tzu had never seen anything so beautiful. Then, all of a sudden, the pedals wilted, falling one by one onto the underground lake's surface. As the last petal disappeared, Lao-Tzu shed a single tear. It disappeared into his moustache. Yet soon enough a new lotus flower appeared in the center of the lake. It was even more delicate, even more luminous than the first.

Lao-Tzu said to the monkey:

"Please tell me my friend, what is this amazing place?"

The monkey looked at him mischievously in the way only monkeys can and said:

> *Don't you know? We're inside*
> *your own heart. The flowers are moments*
> *in your life that are born, then die.*
> *You humans, you've found many*
> *ways to measure time, but know this—*
> *life itself is measured in lotus flowers.*

Lao-Tzu remained absorbed by the beauty of the sight
for a long time. He had studied the Way of the ancient
kings, identified just and good ways of conduct, classified
difference and similarity, parsed the natural and the artificial,
understood that the possible was in the end impossible ...
But all of that was mere appearance. He had before him
being in its original form. The monkey said:

When the work is done, it's time to step aside.

As he was leaving the grotto, Lao-Tzu thought he saw the silhouette of the monkey waiting for him, but instead of golden fur, he saw an overcoat made of rags. The mischievous face was now wrinkled with a serious smile. By his dignified appearance, Lao-Tzu recognized his former colleague in Emperor Pingwang's court, the venerable Confucius. Confucius bowed and said:

"Well I've been looking for the Way for fifty years, and I haven't found anything that looks like it."

"Tell me, honorable Confucius," replied Lao-Tzu, "about your search for the Way"

Confucius' smile took on a pained cast.

"I looked for it in ritual and history. I looked for it in art and music. I looked for in books, and with every mathematical approach. I tried the most complex methods, and when they didn't lead anywhere, I dedicated myself to the study of yin and yang."

"If man is just an infinitesimal part of the universe," said Lao-Tzu, "how could he presume to measure it? Reject science, renounce knowledge itself, and look for the peak of emptiness. When you return to the base, you will be at peace, and being at peace is to unite with destiny. Once you have found it, you will know the constant, and knowing the constant is to embrace the universal. Once you have embraced it, you will be royal, and being royal is to reach the heavenly. Whoever is heavenly can be united with the Way."

Confucius sighed:

"Oh, Lao-Tzu, your wisdom is like a dragon's."

"You ask me to show you the Way," continued Lao-Tzu, "but what are we calling the Way? It's important to distinguish heaven's Way from people's way. The Way of heaven is active inaction. People's way is constrained by action. We can't see the Way of heaven from people's way because it is too distant. If we could give the Way as a gift, we would present it to our prince. If we could offer the Way, we would offer it to our parents. If we could transmit the Way, we would transmit it to our children and grandchildren. The knowledge you seek isn't in books, because books were written by other men, and you are searching for heavenly knowledge. Books are prints left by our ancestors. Your own books, oh Confucius, are just prints. A boot leaves a print, but is a print a boot?"

Lao-Tzu sketched the bamboo, the birds, the pebbles around him. They all showed the irrepressible ripening of time toward its fruit:

"Changes affect all beings, but who knows why things change? How can we distinguish all of the possibilities? Where is the beginning? Where is the end?" he asked.

Then he murmured:

"Let's just wait calmly, not moving, like a baby that has yet to smile."

Confucius meditated on these words, and made his reply:

"Birds hatch, fish spawn, butterflies metamorphose. We have kept ourselves apart from these transformations for a long time. How can someone who isn't part of change transform people?"

It is told that Confucius stayed at the entrance of the cave for a whole season. He did not eat any cooked food. In his left hand he held a block of wood, which he hit with a stick, tonelessly singing long-forgotten songs with no melodies. One day, a peasant passed in front of the cave and asked him what he was doing.

"Even silk clothing becomes rags," responded Confucius. "Avoiding heaven's hardships is easy," he said, "but avoiding people's favors is difficult. Every beginning is also an ending. Man and heaven are one."

The peasant scratched his head, thinking he was dealing with a crazy person.

"To understand nothing is to understand everything," whispered Confucius.

The last rays of sunlight feebly lit the arid plain that extended before the border guard Guanyin. The day had been a boring one. Few travelers ventured to this province at the frontier of the Middle Kingdom. A slight shimmer troubled the uniform landscape. Guanyin squinted his eyes and could see a man approaching. He was perched on a water buffalo, kicking up little dust clouds. When the man reached Guanyin, the border guard said:

"Old man, you're hereby leaving the protection of the Son of Heaven. Where are you going, abandoning the land of your ancestors?"

"Let's say that I'm fleeing my disciples. They lay in the shade the all day long, discussing what's hard and what's soft," said the voyager with a smile.

Guanyin could not believe his ears. Could this traveler be the legendary Lao-Tzu, who had been missing for more than half a century? In a trembling voice, he asked:

"Master, are you going to depart and keep your wisdom from the rest of the world?"

"Look at this desert," murmured Lao-Tzu, "look at those sand dunes. Constantly shifting. Can any sage in the world teach you more than the sand and the dunes?"

"Venerable Master," responded Guanyin, prostrating himself, "I am but a poor subject of His Majesty. I spend my free time writing poems and hunting gazelles. My heart, however, is open to beauty. Of course, I have no right to be asking anything of you, but your words could illuminate the deepest reaches of my soul, and I would like to reflect on them once you've gone."

Lao-Tzu thought for a moment, then, without getting off the water buffalo, he agreed to write down some of his thoughts. They would become the collection that he entitled the *Tao Te Ching*, which means the *Classic Book of the Way and of Virtue*. The writing took barely an hour.

When he had finished, he handed the scroll to Guanyin who gladly accepted it.

"Master, may I read it immediately in your presence to make sure I haven't missed any words? Your calligraphy is in the old style."

"Go ahead, my friend. Read it out loud. Read it clearly."